SOUL
SPECTERS

LORENZO DE LUCA

Ordering Information:

Prime Seven Media
518 Landmann St.
Tomah City, WI 54660

Printed in the United States of America

To wild ancient spirits,
may they float adrift
through cosmic mysteries
as entities of luminous energy,
until the never-ending passing of time.

INTRODUCTION

"I write for myself, I write for you, I write for the people, I write to make sense of the useless nonsense of existence and society, I write to feel alive, I write when I'm dead inside, I write to vent, I write to confess, I write to wake you up when you're asleep and I write to keep you awake when you cannot sleep, I write to give you the truth even when I write irrational follies, I write for the youth. I write because I'm a man, I write without a plan, I write lost in time, I write because I'm free and I write because I want to free you and your mind. I write for the spirits hovering in dark nights, fighting low tides. I write for lonely hearts that pray for a life full of love to start. I write for black souls and demons, for old folks with no remorse, for the dead ones above and for those who will come. I write for empathy, emotions and sensations, I write for vibrations. The secret is gone, read it, feel it and then you will know."

This contemporary poetry emerges from a cathartic need to explore the human soul and the existential, universal currents of life. It speaks in fractured rhythms and raw silences, where language becomes both wound and remedy. These poems carry the weight of personal histories and collective memory, of identities in flux and meaning perpetually deferred. In their vulnerability, they become a quiet revolution, confronting emptiness with presence, and despair with a relentless yearning for truth.

What follows is an inner travel through the mysteries of the cosmic and personal existence, intended as a mirror for other souls, so they might reflect their sensations and experiences in these simple verses.

Hoping that empathy will rise in your hearts, rushing through the blood of your pumping veins and feeding the ghosts that reside in your minds.

Welcome.

POEMS OF ECLIPSE

CHAPTER ONE

FALL

Floating leaves,
dancing trees
shaken by the wind.
Crazy stormy sounds
echoing from the clouds.
The ground is yellow, red and green:
sublime autumn atmosphere
that reflects my
falling
soul.

MORTAL MAN

Mortal man
lend me your hand,
your hourglass finished the sand.

Simple man,
too simple to understand
follow me beyond the end,
we will take off,
but never land.

Crazy man
what did you expect?
Death is a mystery you cannot plan.

ILLUSIONS

It is cold outside,
it is hot inside.
I have lost myself
seeing you here by my side.
It is not so wise
to live in a fantasy
and realize
that illusions make you die.

Cry,
lover cry,
only in my mind
your deep lovely eyes I can find.
And I cannot help but try.

GREED

What do you want?
The poor
asked the rich.
I want you to be poor
and I want me to be rich.

What do you want?
The rich
asked the poor.
I do not want you to be poor
and I do not want me to be rich,
I just want you to comprehend
how miserable is your greed.

UNIVERSE

Universe is an entity,
made by flowing energy,
alive and constantly expanding
until entropy writes the ending.

Earth and life are consequences,
laws are clues for comprehending.
Actions and reactions,
atoms interactions,
intergalactic madness
dark matter, unknown sadness.

Strings, frequencies and dimensions,
godly interventions.

DARE

Dare,
youth never comes again.
Dare while you can,
young shining man.
Remember to dare,
death does not care.
Old is late
for your fate
and time is unfair.
Life is too rare,
to live and not to dare.

PARANOID

An infinite flow of thoughts
has got me caught
in a never-ending spiral,
thoughts going viral,
expanding through human minds
and the reactions that I find
leave me alone,
without words.

SANDS

Tidal wave of sand,
mystery with no end.
Secrets, fog and dust,
ocean of mistrust.
Thunderstorm of lust
burns flowers from the past.

Forever it will last.

FALLING STAR

I saw a falling star, oh girl,
it reminded me of the light we shared.
Where did it go?
Disappeared before I could understand.
It left a scar on my skin
and dissolved way too far,
in another galaxy.

The dust, it lasts as energy.
The love, it fades into eternity.

STRANGER

Hey you, beautiful stranger,
girl I do not know,
lost in the night,
under the moonlight.
Forever and ever,
always and never,
known and unknown.
I hope you can reflect your gentle soul
in these words I recall:
you cannot reach the highest heights
if you do not touch the deepest lows.

VOID

To fill
my interior void
I choose
everything I avoid.
Still
I loose,
treating
every choice
as a deafening
silent noise.

GREY MATTER

All is grey
outside.
Smoke blowing
inside
my burning mind.
I am lost.
I search, but never find
what I need the most.
Confusing clouds of doubt
covered the light of my sun,
the only glare, I dare not live without.
So, I run and I run
escaping the foggy places of my brain,
breaking the chains
that kept me in pain.

DESERT

Desert of sadness.
I grab some sand,
but I cannot keep it in my hand.
What a terrible mess:
holding the truth
and all its proofs
and still may not confess.

FLAMES OF EYES

I need to feel
that heat
deep down
in my soul.
Starting from my knees
ending on my cheeks,
without it I do not breathe.
Raise my flames
and rise.
Burn me
like the sun,
with the power of your eyes.

DOOM

Years
and years
of pain.
I cry
with the sky
sweet tears of rain.
I shall not hide
from my doom,
my life is a tide
and you are the moon.

COSMIC CITIES

City lights
shine bright
like stars in the sky,
on dark hills,
in the wild
blind
night.
Fusing earth and galaxies
into cosmic universal towns.

MYSTERY

A charming mystery
at the edge of the horizon,
where the red bloody clouds
kiss the waves
of the deep blue ocean.
There,
with love,
I die.

TEARS

Burning eyes
crying melancholic salted tears
anytime you are not near.
And a giant void
of pure sad nothing
filled with lies.

DEADLY FLOWERS

Deadly flowers
over tombs of bones.
Graves of past existences
echoing into eternity.
Passing away memories.

FORBIDDEN LOVE

Forbidden love,
I will meet you in another lifetime.
When we both will be
universal matter,
dark and unknown.

LIFT

The smog
jumbles
up with the fog,
humble
winds whisper
to the mist
in the grey
grey nothing.
And the spirit
of Mother Earth
lifts.

WIND

The wind
is whispering cold
in this slow gentle night,
the echo resonates,
to give us life,
to give us wings
that will carry our light,
casting away
the shadows of our minds.

AWAY

Far,
by car,
away,
which way?
Don't know,
but go,
today.
Past
is a scar,
it lasts,
dirty like dust.
Forget and forgive.
Leave,
grieve.
Live,
believe,
so many futures to achieve.
Too many pleasures to give
and joys to receive.
Life is to live.

INVISIBLE

I am the darkness
I am the storm
I am the soul of a black night,
the absence of the light,
the evil death of white,
the deep silence inside.
I am the shadows
I am the burning fire,
the wild spirit of blind lies.
I am all the things invisible to your eyes.

REST

Your wet eyelids
left me.
A touch of evil,
desperation
and nostalgia
possessed me,
a melancholic sensation
rising down my chest.
Rest,
forever,
blooming flower.

TIME CRIMES

Sometimes, always, never,
words and emotions last forever.
Wherever,
whenever,
spaces and times,
passages of lives,
reading through the lines.
Never-ending entropy,
universal crimes.

LIGHT

You are the light
infinitely bright.
Explosion in the night sky
super massive stars collide.
Too luminous,
drives me blind.
Continuous
shining of a kind
luster, time after time.
Enlightened by,
I will never
ever hide.

Darkness left my side.

VAMPIRE LOVER

Kill me
to give me life,
stab me
with a sharped knife.
Lick my blood
immortal lover,
little vampire.
Your violence
increases my desire,
you are the fire,
that burns and inspires.
The sweet moments
of red pain
are the only ones
where my masochistic soul can feel alive.
I love you the most when you are a fucking liar.
Drink all my spirit
from my dry veins,
until oblivion
and tell me you want to love me
for the rest of our time,
for the rest of the times.

ECLIPSE

I have been sun
I have been moon
I have been eclipsed
I have been dark
I have been drunk
I have been poison
I have been fuel
I have been cruel
I have been flames
I have been shames
I have been mad
I have been sad
I have been dead
I have been damned.

Now I just start it all over again
in this not reversable cycle of pain
called life.

BLACK HOLE

Black hole
inside my soul.
Fall
into my gravity.

END

Where are we going?
Lost in grey clouds of smoke
and green carpets of trash and money.

Where are we going?
Souls of nature,
specters of the earth.

When is it all going to end?
Broken, unrepairable hearts,
telepathic burning heads,
collective consciousness.

Darkness over light,
heat and melting ice,
living not so wise.

I will wait for the red sun
over hills of frustrated peace.

I will wait and watch the flames
eating everything.

GHOST POEMS

CHAPTER TWO

TELEPATHY

We are now living
in a wild telepathic world and society.
Your heads are radios,
old movie machines and projectors,
new multigenetic, modern electrical appliances
ready to be used until the end of fun.

The waves are taking control over everything
inside our unharmed minds.
Waves of uncontrollable thoughts,
tides of madness
that not even the moon can influence.

The man is compulsively connected to the television
or to a certain frequency
coming from everywhere:
voices, radio stations, songs,
spots, computers, social networks, telephones
and even movies…
Reality is burning and deteriorated.
Fake news and misinformation rule this chaos
generating ignorance and stupidity.
Pure manipulation
of malleable brains
and thought control.
Everything is about to fall.

People are floating around
like ghost entities, disconnected,
uncapable of any demonstration of what real life is,
searching for a stupid kind of momentary pleasure.
In this new unconscious era
the only real reason to be alive is to feel.
To have true sensations,
emotions
and personal opinions.
Think with your own mind
and go find a lover,
you stupid robots.

CONFESSION

Starting my confession:
I had an observation
that led me to depression,
losing all the passion.
The power of creation
is my true obsession,
related to connections
and sharing inspiration.
Intuition
and elevation.
I traveled every nation
without a real direction,
station after station,
to land in desolation.
Spirituality became my profession,
giving love my mission,
leaving all possessions
searching truths and revelations.
Culture contaminations
free my mind from segregations,
artistic infatuation
knowing that knowledge is confrontation.
Alone in damnation.
Mirrors and reflections,
projected fake distractions,
mind contortions and defections.
Burning frustration,
freedom oppression.

DNA manipulation
and modification,
voices and manifestations.

God, forgive me and my condition,
because there is no medication.
God, give me levitation,
then I can leave this abomination.

LAWS OF THINKING

I thought
I was thinking
In a sort of right
way of thinking.
Suddenly I was blinded by the light
and my memory forgot.
All my experiences became vain.
Truths and laws
I could not explain,
cause I had no proofs to show,
even if existence appeared tremendously bright:
visualizing with brain
and not with eyesight.

And you, gentle
madame
made me
realize
how crazy became life
when you read my mind,
predicting line
after line
the disorder I have inside.
Paranoia possessed me,
growing like an infinite tree,
changing my vision of seeing things.
Turning my persona into a madness ill machine.

GHOST

Hope
is what I lost
living as a ghost.
Dope
is what I found,
lost into the sound
of this crazy silence bounds.
Around and around
just to end up underground.
Life is a twisted dream,
it begins
when you fall asleep.
Wake up and see
how it seems
to feel for ever stuck, in reality.

I will reach the next dimension
with pure feelings of ascension,
godly love and death intervention.

LOOP

Oh my, oh my
the loop I'm inside
it never ends,
it makes me cry.
And I do not know why
time makes me shy,
day after day,
lie after lie.
Mayday, mayday
my brain is going down,
crashing like a plane
and there is nothing I can say.
No way, no way
I must not get out.
I shout
without
the noise
of my voice.
The cycle restarts
and I have no choice
but falling apart.

INNER TRAVEL

Waterfall of sadness,
flames of madness.
Where do I find joy?
I shall go somewhere,
maybe I will swim down
the whole river bed,
to drown in a lake,
led
by the currents of mistake.
Strangers
acting strange
and fake.
I grow abandoned in nature,
but I am not mature
enough
to walk alone through the dark.
Embark
with me
on a lonely trip
inside each other's minds,
to see what we find.
Maybe I am just traveling my interior ways,
the places where my consciousness lays.
Maybe I am just talking to myself,
like the sea whispers into the shells.

Be kind
to yourself
when you
have a conversation
with you
in your head.

CHAOS

Living nonsense
to make some sense,
sensing irrational lies
to feed rational truths.
Contradiction is my clue.

Frustration kills freedom
déjà vu
after déjà vu.
Nothing but boring boredom.
Nevertheless
I love the obsession of being obsessed
with this hateful awful stress.
Tension is too intense,
closes relief behind a fence.

Chaos in my case,
I need harmony to face
this crazy mad, mad phase.

Breathe and move.
Forward.

CHAINS

Slavery, chains.
Frustration, pain.
Always the same game:
ghosted by spirits until I go insane
with no one to really blame.
Do not know how to stop the rain,
pretending that all is real,
when all is fake.
The undefeatable power to be damned.

A change must come to life.
Now rain is knocking at my window again,
ticking on the ground.
Wet, teared,
melancholic comforting sound.
Now I embrace the dead and their cries,
the living and their lies.
The decisive power of a free man
daydreaming of liberty plans.

INSANE

Chained,
withheld,
suspended,
trapped,
imprisoned
in mine and other entities,
existences,
afterlife.
I see what is hidden,
sense what is forbidden
and hear what specters want me to listen.
Signs of tender life
and harsh death,
visions,
hallucinations,
stars and burning flames.
Insane.

FREQUENCY

Mind elevation
based on connections,
riding the wave,
going on air.
Using our telepathic brain
to feel the energy from miles away,
discovering the real way.
There is a neural net,
it expands.
What do you get?
It depends.

Tune into the right frequency.
The Universe will bless your destiny.

LOVELY HATE

Loving is a crime
killed by pride and time,
I will gently whisper a secret in your ear:
to clearly clean my fear
I am pretending that I am fine.

My eyes are burning salt
yet I cannot shed a single tear.
What a frustrating fault,
to keep all the hate inside, my dear.

Your shadow follows
my steps and ways
as I fall in hollows
of obscure days.
Miserable fate
of lovely hate.

SPIRIT

Never underestimate the strength
of your true spirit,
your inner speaker,
your lover
and believer.

Most of the time
of our dying lives
that powerful resonating energy
stays asleep,
down deep
in lethargy.

It awakens with love,
blessing from above,
infinite potential
of an exponential
super massive burning star
coming from too far.

A constant explosion
flowing
and lighting
and growing
like emotions.

Open your eyes
and rise.

DEMONS

Demons surrounding,
frightening
nightmares,
spectral adventures.

Trapped in walls,
giving up the springtime
to welcome the fall
of my mortal soul.

Trespassing
doors of hell,
gates of damnation,
to dwell
there for ever
and never
cling to salvation.

Devil was waiting for me,
my whole life.
Devil saw my sins all the time,
and now claims to be my wife.

It tastes so delicious,
the evil touch delirious
of the warm flames
of shames
flaring up in Inferno.

SHADOWS

Shadows,
dark projections
of hunting ghosts,
uninvited hosts.

Foggy presences
hiding,
skulking,
lurking.
Consequences
of light,
invisible at night.

Days of shadows.
Days of being lost
days of thinking,
days of nothing.

DISAPPEAR

Lover,
leave.
Disappear.
Do not ever dare to cross my mind again,
as my tears flow into a river of black dirty rain,
as a thunder shares its light,
echoing through the night.
And never reappear
as a memory or ghost.
I need to make it clear:
you will nevermore be my host,
fantasy nor real.

WOLF

Leave me,
without a single word.
I am a lone wolf
wandering for the woods of the world,
howling songs of a blind doom,
waiting for the next full moon.
Soon,
let me know
when the moment comes for me
to set you free
and give you life again,
in this crazy circle of pain.

ALONE

I
was alone.
Loner
on every corner.
Me
in every street.
Myself
through heaven and hell.
Person
in prison,
imprisoned
in my persona.

Everybody
is nobody,
no one
is everyone.
All of us use
to confuse
and to lose
ourselves,
just spells
into nothingness.

Man,
Woman,
strange
strangers.

We
are never
together.

Life
is one.
A lonely
loner one,
until death comes.
Dead
is not alive,
but still alone.
Mad
is to live,
yet you're gone.

FAREWELL

The cold kisses
of your snowy lips,
the burned wishes
of your dancing hips.
I forgot to remember
to die with you.
December
and nothing new.
The last year
of our stupid fear
to be us, to be clear.
Separated
souls,
now
divided
we grow.
Ready to meet
when our feet
lift.
Sky will be my latest gift,
as on this earth there is nothing more to tell.
Farewell.

DRUNK

Dark,
drunk
nights
and fights.
Specters of the cities
hovering
in noisy silence,
owning
their duties
of deadly presence.
Cheers
to mortal life.
Crack a bottle and shake a knife.
Cheers
to forgotten memories.
Echoes of moans, like melodies.
The day is made to sleep,
even six feet deep.
The moon
is made to howl, loon.

It is a twisted dreamy nightmare, to die for a living.

THE CURRENTS
OF EXISTENCE

CHAPTER THREE

I SOUGHT YOU AT NIGHT

I sought you at night
through the streets of the world,
in the disappointing desolation.
I found you in the dream
of a future existence,
of an everlasting illumination.
And by day, there was darkness.
But in sleep I saw
all that my eyes
would never have shown me.
Lost in the oneiric abyss
of infinite love
for a fallen angel.

MOON

For long I gazed at the moon,
like a sailor seeking the lighthouse,
like a lone wolf, fierce and cursed,
like a specter begging for fortune.

I am a wave that flows and breaks,
a tear falling from a weeping face,
I am the sea's water rising
until it drowns me.

I am the tide of the human soul,
ebbing and swelling for a stolen kiss,
for a snatched away glance,
for the gentle caress of a tender hand.

For long I gazed at the moon
and the astral tides have broken me,
yet I still hope the sun will never rise again, condemned
to gaze forever at the cold, distant, pale moon.

I EXTINGUISHED THE WIND

I extinguished the wind
with the fire that raged within,
burned
in a senseless March sunset, spurned.
And I stole time from mighty Cronos.
Vengeance struck, loud and dire
with blinding flare,
his thunder laid bare.
I beg for grace, I kneel and pray,
arrogant in my disarray.
Now I am a chained, defeated man
enslaved by my most wretched sin:
the unbearable presumption
to master what defies all assumption.

NAKED

Naked
before the mirror,
in the young reflection made old
by your raw flesh.
You look at yourself, unable
to grasp how fleeting the body is,
and how deceiving its shape.
What stays hidden within
decides your heaven and your hell.
You see what you want to see, just how you want it,
not what you need,
which at all you cannot see.

DEAD

Dead,
I surrender to the reaper's hands,
to my grave carved deep in the arid sands
of a desert where no wind dares cry,
where truth and form dissolve and lie,
where all is nothing, drifting by.

For I am alive,
each day
in a world that dies.
And I am dead,
each night
in the depths where the heart denies.

Farewell, forsaken love,
buried, hidden, left unloved.

MADNESS

Sane distracted madness,
splattered like abstract paint,
hysterical and desperately insane.
Brushstrokes of blood, raging lunacy,
murderous paintings like visions
in the languid mind
possessed by possessions.
Sweetly
killing the enemies of fiery combustions,
we were born for destruction.
I hate the dullness of sanity's
crust, which conforms like an idiosyncratic banality,
while the illness deserves reality.
From the mad, I learned how to live.
From the sane, I learned only: all must give.
Sooner or later
we all perish, polished and traitorous.

HUMAN

I dreamed I was a human being
in some forgotten age, unseen,
craving war
to conquer more,
lusting for power
to crown my will in every hour.
Greed consumed my very core
in every stage
of foolish evolution's lore,
no matter what the flag or shore.
Everywhere, ravenous beasts hungry for extinction.

I woke, I was the devil, bearer of depraved damnation,
of corrupted, cursed upheaval.
But still I slept,
anxious for a future lewd and lethal.

I declared myself a living flame,
Lucifer by name,
blazing through the needed and the vain,
the necessary and the ephemeral,
the flesh and the spiritual.

And so it was, and ever shall it be:
man alone is true demon, endlessly.

NOW

Foolish,
not to grasp the now.
Now, we become
forever
what we can never be
again.

I hate you
because I cannot love you
in this useless instant,
this moment far away.
The present slips from me;
the second I name it,
it's already gone.

Farewell, my concubine,
farewell, bitter joy.
We will be the sky's own tears
but never cry
a second flood.

Farewell, forgotten ones:
the drifting, indifferent,
mistrusting all who breathe.
You dwell in endless yesterdays,
awaiting futures
that will never arrive.

Now has never been
and never will be.

TOGHETHER

Together we will go against the lukewarm currents.
Together we will feel the warmth of the dying,
freezing, shivering before the icy living.
Together we will react to the insolent cowardice
of unconscious liars,
to the abuses of power
of greedy wretched incoherent men.
Alone, we will unite to defend ourselves against changes
wrought by miserable indecents,
to the harm of innocents.
Beware!
Lonely and powerless men,
together hearts ignite and sleepers dare to wake.
Together we will dance upon the crumbling ruins
of these merciless oppressive civilizations,
to found together, radiant reborn societies.

I TURNED MY BACK

I turned my back
on your smiling face of treachery
that stormed my guts,
lifted me off the ground,
filled my chest with warm sirocco,
looked at me melting my limbs,
looked at me throwing lightning
and fear, of never meeting again.
I turned proudly,
with the courage of one who does not face remorse,
to never turn back again.
And inside was the emptiest void
and then nothing more.

SURVIVE

Survive,
may the light enfold you
in golden swaddles,
gentle newborn.
Rage
beyond the darkest gloom of existence
and rejoice in the sparkling summer nights
of your carefreeness.
Grow,
spread your earthly roots
until they touch the weary clouds
that fly and cry.
Cry with them
when the storms of the soul
will pour down in flashing bursts
to stab your heart.
Endure
the cowardly locked doors
of immature maturities,
the whims of those
who have already won
yet still long to see you fall.
Survive
the deadly aged terrors:
may the afterlife not bury you,
but lead you into new universal mysteries.

FOREVER

Forever,
you whispered,
with trembling voice
and burning brow,
feverish with emotions
that dare not imagine an end.
Clinging to the idea
of an everlasting embrace.

GALAXY

The galaxy was immense
and shone with soft gaseous hues,
variegated, painted by impressionists.
To float in the memories of stars,
to drift in the unknown milky ocean,
where spirits are energetic waves,
where ancient lights are echoes of time,
where eternity gravitates immortal.
And thus, lost in creation
and in the ethereal inconclusiveness of deciphering it,
I surrendered myself to alienation.

SUBLIME

Sublime
to feel a landscape
that speaks in sorrow,
that steals the breath away
like a gasping cry,
to listen to it and behold it
in the explosive silence.
From the ethereal height of the peaks
to the black abyssal depths,
my swooning body
imprisons a force
that presses
and presses still,
just to break free and see.

BEYOND

You lost me
along the faintest paths
drawn by destiny,
in the vain attempt
to accompany me home
with your naive, perpetual hope,
but I did not want to return
to Ithaca,
I wished to sink,
to be shipwrecked, to plunge
into the incurable sickness of the sea.
And now that the Fates
have cut my thread,
I die with an unbridled longing
for you.
I will wait for you
beyond time,
beyond the world,
and our journey
shall never end.

THE TREE OF LIFE

The tree of life,
born from the seed of discord,
gives pure air to lungs suffocated by concrete,
nourishes with new sap the withered still lifes
in cycles altered by toxic clouds and industrial chemicals.
From bare branches,
foolish men will fall in droves,
when the untamable fires
will blaze to engulf everything.
And the dense smoke and sooty ash
will become bitter clouds in winter's dimmed sky.
The roots of evil were planted
by selfish descendants
of the tree of life,
who now watch helpless,
while it burns with more flames than the sun.

FORBIDDEN YOUTH

(FINAL VISUAL CHAPTER)

CROOKED MOON

To ask the night
for mysteries
the moon shall not clarify,
and to die
beneath the damp veil of lies
that dew
makes bloom again.

Copenhagen, 2024

HOOD

Life slips away,
like sand
through my fingers,
ephemeral,
untouchable.

Greedy,
I grow rich
on desperate sensations.

Copenhagen, 2024

DESTINIES

Through fleeting meetings,
diverging paths,
distant crossings,
and passing glances,
through indifferent thoughts
and hesitant hearts,
our roads are drawn,
sketched by a trivial fate.

IMMENSE

I find new meaning
in the vast unknown,
submerged
in the sky's quiet tears.
And it feels as though
even the universe
can weep
honest and alone.
Yet all things flow,
they rise,
and start anew
more alive,
more real,
more true.

Berlin, 2022

THE SKY OVER BERLIN

The vastness opened, the sky, the universe,
in an autumn park,
where earth reached for sunlit clouds,
lovers on the horizon.
And life surged, electric,
through the quiet rapture
of a cyclist
learning how to fly.

Budapest, 2025

HOPE

Hope,
do not fade,
dazzle.
Awaken the sleepers
abandoned in darkness.
Grant me a flash
and the crash of thunder,
an electric charge
that shakes my senses.
The light
guides me
into every hidden corner of shadow.

Vienna, 2025

MUSEUM

May the world become
the museum of your dreams.
Art lives in every place we perceive it,
as a reflection of our very soul

Berlin, 2022

OUTLAW

I survive
my own fate,
relapsing
like an outlaw
always fleeing,
always aching,
elusive,
self-defeating.
Only escape
makes me feel alive.

Berlin, 2022

WALL

To shatter the wall
with roaring TNT,
with the blast of raw dynamite.
To see the rubble float
in November's dull grey
for the ecstasy of blazing rebels.
Fireworks.
Bombs like thunder
freeing shackled spirits,
the glittering delirium of destruction
echoes through the vast blueprint of revolutions.
To tear down the wall
with the bleeding foreheads
of the furious oppressed,
just to see what lies
on the other side of freedom.

Munich, 2022

MELANCHOLIA

Melancholic melancholia
of having crossed
the borders of my blooming,
mature being.
The sands in the hourglass
refuse to slow their frantic fall,
and all flows faster,
more unstoppable.
From the steepest peaks
at the height of existence,
I will wait, anxious,
for the wheezing slowdown
born of tedious old age.
Forever fugitive, trapped
in deceiving phases,
in the slow and swift revolutions
of this moon-drunk carousel.

Brussels, 2022

NIGHT OVER BRUSSELS

Starry night, blind and still.
The city dazzles like a vain galaxy.
Every corner, every street, every way
shines to gift us moments of drunken longing.
Eternal, it never sleeps
and only light remains in the dark.

Brussels, 2022

CITY

The city smiles
at lost spirits,
wraps them,
welcomes them,
makes them vividly alive.
It offers shelter
to evasive
and fleeing minds.
It dazzles and shines,
consumes
and devours,
wears down
and deteriorates.
Ambivalent and incoherent,
lover
and whore.
It embraces and abandons,
nurtures and withers,
allows and forbids.

Italy, 2025

NIGHTMARE

Demonic slaughter,
a crawling murder
within my weary, shattered mind,
frozen, black visions of funeral endings,
of untimely burials.
I sink underground,
torn apart by rage,
cut and sold like an animal.
And breath comes hard,
corroded
by doom.
My nightmare haunts me, night and day,
drowning all desire
to savor
the best years of my life.

Munich, 2022

WATCH OVER US

Watch over us
with courage
in the dawn-lit nights
of battle,
in bitter wars,
in the unguarded moments
of gentle souls.
Protect
the shining spirits,
and your light
will never fade.

Italy, 2025

STREETS

Through the streets,
where the scent of people overwhelms you,
I fought,
at night,
with corrupted souls,
with the taste of iron in my mouth,
with a fearless heart
and a twisted stomach.
I closed the doors to life
and flung them wide open to death.
Reopening every ancient wound
to make love
with my cold fate.